HOW DOES UNIVERSITY WORK?

CONNOR WHITELEY

No part of this book may be reproduced in any form or by any electronic or mechanical means. Including information storage, and retrieval systems, without written permission from the author except for the use of brief quotations in a book review.

This book is NOT legal, professional, medical, financial or any type of official advice.

Any questions about the book, rights licensing, or to contact the author, please email connorwhiteley@connorwhiteley.net

Copyright © 2023 CONNOR WHITELEY

All rights reserved.

DEDICATION
Thank you to all my readers without you I couldn't do what I love.

INTRODUCTION

When we all first think about going to university (and when we are still at university for that matter) we always have tons of questions about how does it work, what it is like and more.

Therefore, when I started blogging for the e-learning platform *Active Class* in June 2021, I really wanted to tackle these questions to help students and thankfully tons of people have found it very useful.

Now I'm putting it into a book so it can help even more people and this book really will as it will cover a lot of topics and questions that both brand new and current university students have about university.

And thankfully it covers a wider range of topics for different students' needs. For example, it covers topics that you might need to know before you go to university. Like how does it work, what is clearing and what are your accommodation options?

Also it covers topics and questions that you

might have when you're at university and in your third year and beyond.

Personally, I cannot stress enough how badly I wish I had a book like this when I was starting off at university. I would have loved to have answers to my questions in a very easy-to-understand, conversational and interesting book.

Believe me, this is nothing like a boring textbook we all know and love as students.

Who Is This Book For?

I know I market this book as a university guide for psychology students, but it really can help anyone who is thinking of coming to university for the first time. Since it really does help them to answer their questions in a simple easy to understand way.

Also if you're just gone to university or have been there for a year or two. This guide is still great for you because it addresses options about your possible future and things that might help you during your time at university.

As well as instead of having to search the internet for hours trying to find your answers, they're all in one place in this book, so that will definitely save you time.

Overall, this is for anyone who wants an interesting conversational guide to your burning university questions.

Who Am I?

Personally I always like to know who writes the nonfiction I'm reading so I know the information is coming from a good source.

Therefore, I'm Connor Whiteley, the author of over 30 psychology books and the host of The Psychology World Podcast, available on all major podcast apps and YouTube, where each week we discuss psychology news and a different psychology topic that you don't learn in the classroom or lectures.

And most importantly for this book, I am a psychology student at the University of Kent, England studying Psychology With Clinical Psychology and A Placement Year. In other words, I specialise in mental health and I have a year's work experience as part of my degree.

So I do know the sort of questions and experiences that university students have.

Now we know each other, let's crack on with learning how does university work.

PART ONE: BEFORE STARTING UNIVERSITY

HOW DOES UNIVERSITY WORK?

IS UNIVERSITY RIGHT FOR YOU?

It seemed only right to start off this book with this chapter because it so fundamental. A lot of great people insist that everyone should go to university, and as much as I agree with them, I really want this book to be balanced. Since I also know that university isn't right for everyone.

Therefore, in case you're thinking about going to university but you aren't sure, then this chapter should definitely help you decide.

As well as even if you're sure that you are going to university, please read it too because I've probably dropped in a tip or two for you as well.

Enjoy!

<u>Is University Right For You?</u>

Whilst a lot of the blog is focused on university students, I know there are some secondary or high school students who look here to. As well as I know from my experience lots of students at this age wonder whether they should go to university or not.

That's the focus on today's blog.

<u>Is University Right For You?</u>

In all honesty my full answer isn't given here because this is a massive topic and I need to be balanced.

Therefore, the entire point of this blog post is to help you decide whether university is right for you or not by starting to get you thinking about some the questions you need to ask yourself.

<u>What's Your Ideal Life?</u>

I want to borrow a concept from my writer self for a moment because it's extremely useful here. As a writer (As with any career) you need to decide what's your ideal creative life and create an action plan to get to it and this takes a number of years but this idea of your ideal creative life helps you make decisions about your writing career.

The exact same goes for university and your life. What type of life do you want?

If you want a certain type of career or you feel like you need a degree. Then university might be for you so go for it.

If you don't want a career or just don't want to go to university, then don't. That's perfectly okay.

I would take a piece of paper and write out where you want YOUR (not someone else's dream of your life) life to be in ten or twenty years and plot a course on how to get there. If you need a degree or a high paid job then university might be for you.

Personally, my ideal life involves psychology and

helping people with their mental health so I need a degree to work in psychology, so university was for me in that sense.

Is it for you?

What is Your Attitude Towards Learning?

Of course, not all of university is about learning. Lots of it is about culture, making new friends, socialising and having fun, but a fair amount of it is about learning.

If you love learning and have a topic you're passionate about then university can be an amazing way for you to explore that topic deeper.

For example, another reason why I went to university is because I love psychology and I really wanted to deepen my knowledge about it. Therefore, I made sure I could satisfy my love of learning and studying so university was a great fit for me there.

A simple question for yourself here is:

Can I see myself wanting to study this topic in (extreme) depth for the next three years?

If the answer's no, then maybe university isn't for you.

What Job Do You Want?

This is where the need for balance comes from because there are some jobs and areas where there are degrees but I really don't see the point in them. And that's all I'm going to say on that issue.

However, if you want a particular job where a degree is absolutely necessary then one of two things will happen. You'll want to go to university because you really want that job and career. Or you might want to re-evaluate how much you want that job because you don't want to go to university.

Both are fine.

I know lots of people who thought they wanted to go to university to do a particular job to change their mind later on.

Therefore, when it comes to deciding if you want to go to university or not, consider what are the job requirements of your ideal job.

For me, I have to have multiple degrees to work in psychology because of the scientific nature and knowledge base that job requires. As well as I'm more than happy to go to university so this wasn't a problem.

Yet if I wanted to work in construction, writing or business. I would probably not go for a degree.

Conclusion:

Overall, in this short blog post we've only barely scratched the surface of this question because it's so big. Yet ultimately you need to make your own decision about if you want to go to university because it's your life and future.

I hope I've started to get you thinking about what you want.

Whatever you decide, I know it'll be right for you.

Good luck on your university journey regardless of how long it is.

HOW DOES UNIVERSITY WORK?

I'm extremely glad that I finally get to address this chapter to psychology student specifically. Since as a psychology student myself this is what my experience is based on and I really wish I had a guide like this when I was going to university. It would have been great to hear another psychology student's perspective.

So I really hope this is useful for you and it answers at least some of the questions you currently have (and if not, it's an interesting read anyway!)

<u>How Does University Work?</u>

When I was investigating possible topics for my blog posts, I was surprised to come across lots of students type *how does university work?* Into google. Now I was surprised because after being in the university bubble for so long, you sort of forget that other people don't know what it's like. Therefore, the point of this post is to help you understand university on a larger level and then I might explore the more niche areas and how they work in future posts.

How Does University Work?

Something that's always fun about writing blog posts is when you sit down to write a topic, it's only then you start to realise how large a particular topic is, but I'll break down how university works as best I can.

Undergraduate Degree Structure

For the purposes of this post, I'm completely ignoring the Masters and PhD degrees because these are higher types of degrees and I'm not sure on the ins and outs of them.

However, an undergraduate degree is typically 3 or 4 years long depending on the degree and it typically works in the following ways:

- Each year is called a Stage at university (for some bizarre reason)
- You need to get a score of 40 or above each year to move onto the next stage.
- Your first year doesn't count towards your degree classification.

You can think of your classification as your overall grade and the first year is both great and bad that it doesn't count as part of your overall classification. It's great because everyone is learning how university works and some students have never done the degree topic before, so they're learning the topic from scratch.

It's bad because the first year is a step down from your 16-18 education (whatever it is in your country) so it's easier. Meaning students tend to do very well that year, so it's annoying that those high grades don't count towards your final classification.

Additionally, I need to mention that whilst getting a score of 40 each year is a pass, it isn't a good pass and it isn't what you need to get into Masters and other higher education programmes. Consequently, what I'm saying is, is don't aim for a pass mark, you might want to try aiming higher.

Some other points are:
- A university year is broken up into three terms.
- In the UK, the Autumn Term runs from late September to Mid December, Spring Terms runs from January to April and the Summer term runs from May to June.

Then a good thing about these terms is there are month long breaks in between each of them, so it gives you a chance to have a break, catch up on learning or do other things in-between.

Going Deeper

As I write this I really feel like I'm talking too generally but the thing about this blog post is unlike the others, this is really aimed at students who are thinking of going to university and are wondering how it all works. Therefore, of course, it would feel to me as if I'm talking too generally.

But now we're going to dive into the weeds and smaller details of how university works:

- Your degree year is broken up into modules (think of these as units or topics)
- Each module is assessed
- You can have optional modules.

Now modules are actually surprisingly interesting to talk about because in the UK, each academic (university) year, you need to have 120 credits and believe me you don't need to worry or even think about credits at all.

In all honesty, I'm not sure on the point of them.

In addition, each module is given a number of credits it is worth, and they tend to be 15 credits for a module that runs for 1 term (either in the Autumn or Spring term), or 30 credits for a module that runs both terms.

For example, in my first year of university, I had three modules that ran for both terms, giving me 90 credits, and I had a compulsory 15 credit module. Then I had 15 credits leftover.

Leading me onto another aspect of modules, some of your modules will be compulsory and this depends on your degree. For instance, if your degree topic has to be accredited (approved) by a professional body like psychology does, then you will probably find you have a lot of compulsory modules so the degree can be accredited.

Other modules will be optional.

Therefore, in my first year, I have had 30 credits "leftover" meaning I could take one 15 credit module that was available to me.

Personally, I love optional (or wild as my university calls them) modules because they allow you to explore areas beyond your degree. Such as, I took a forensic psychology (which isn't profiling!) module because I was interested in that area.

However, you don't have to take optional modules from your degree topic. Since for my final year I am seriously considering taking a module in something akin to Entertainment Law as I know that will be useful for me in the future. But as you can tell Entertainment Law is very different from psychology.

Yet that's the point I'm trying to make, university allows you to customise your degree to various extents so it's useful to you and you get to have fun.

<u>Conclusion:</u>

As I write this I have a massive smile on my face because I know for a fact I have only scratched the surface of how does university work. There are a lot more nuanced pieces, like assignments, grades and everything, but I hope this blog post has allowed you to understand university a little more, and hopefully you have learnt something.

Personally, I do love university and it has been great for me, so whatever you decide to do, I wish you the best of luck.

HOW TO CHOOSE THE RIGHT SPECIFIC DEGREE FOR YOU?

I am honestly shocked that I have reached a certain point by chapter 3 of the book. I always knew there would come a time where I would struggle to put these chapters into a logical order because all of these are so important and interconnected.

I just hoped I wouldn't be struggling this early on!

Therefore, the rest of the chapters for this part of the book will be in a very solid and the closest I could get to a perfectly logical and chronological order.

But they're all still extremely useful like this next chapter that you might not have thought of before.

<u>How To Choose The Right Specific Degree For You?</u>

I fully admit this is a strange topic because most people, before they start to think about going to university, tend to think a biology degree (for example) is just that. A biology degree and nothing else. But at several universities lots of degrees can be divided up into different types and specialisations for the same topic. Therefore, in this blog post I'm going to explain what are the benefits and how to choose the specific degree for you?

What Are The Different Types of Degrees?

I'm not talking about degrees like Bachelors, Masters and PhDs. Instead I'm talking about universities that offer a range of different degrees for the same topic. For example, I study psychology and at my university there are the following undergraduate degrees for psychology:

- Psychology
- Psychology with Clinical Psychology
- Psychology With Clinical Psychology and A Placement Year (My One!)
- Psychology With A Year Aboard
- Psychology With A Placement Year
- And on and on and on…

There's easily another four psychology degrees that I could add.

Therefore, as you can see there are a lot of options and my university isn't the only one who offer lots of choices for students. Leading us to the question of how do you choose?

What Are The Benefits of Doing Different Degree?

Generally speaking, there are a lot of benefits to doing the other degrees instead of the normal ones. For example, I chose *Psychology With Clinical Psychology and A Placement* Year because I wanted to do psychology but I wanted extra experience in clinical psychology and I wanted real-life work experience as part of my degree.

Meaning as a result of doing a more specialised degree, I get extra knowledge about clinical psychology which I would not have gotten if I did a normal Psychology degree, and I get a year's work experience built-in as part of my degree. Both these things will hopefully benefit me in the job market in the future.

As a result whenever it comes to choosing the type of degree you want, you need to look at the benefits it gives you. For instance, if I wanted to go into Forensic Psychology, I would choose a psychology degree with that focus as it'll give you more experience and knowledge of the topic at an undergraduate level.

What Do You Want?

I know I mention this often but this is critical, what do you want from your degree?

What knowledge or achievements do you want at the end of your degree?

This is even more critical than choosing the topic of your degree because deciding what you want will help decide the type of degree you want.

For example, at the end of my degree, I wanted:

- An understanding of psychology.
- An understanding of clinical psychology.
- Work experience to help stand out in the future job market.

Therefore, a normal psychology degree was fairly useless for me because I would have an understanding of psychology, but not clinical or work experience. At least not part of my degree.

Equally, forensic psychology or degrees with A Year Abroad wouldn't benefit me too much. Since as much as I love the idea of A Year Aboard, I just don't think it's for me.

Meaning the degree type I choose was the only one that would allow me to do what I wanted.

However, you could be different. You might love the idea of living and learning in another country for a year. If so, explore A Year Aboard option with your degree.

If you love a specific area of your degree subject then see if there's a degree with specialist modules in that area.

The Real Point of The Chapter

The real point of this blog post isn't to talk about the specifics of these specific degrees. The real point is to make you aware and open your eyes to the fact that a degree isn't a degree. A degree is whatever you want it to be.

Therefore, if you wanted your degree to be a normal one, fine. That's amazing and I wish you all the luck in the world with it.

But if you want to do something different with your degree, be it a placement year, a Year Aboard, specialised modules, then go out and look for it. You might never know what you'll find.

Will it be easy?

Probably not.

In all honesty, I'm only aware of these different types of degrees because I stumbled across them on my university's website and they were mentioned on Open Days.

Am I pleased I found them?

Definitely!

I love my choice of degree, because now I get to do psychology with a focus (mainly in my final year) on clinical psychology, which I love. Also as I write this I get to work with great people on great projects that I never would have been able to work on otherwise without my placement.

All because I took a chance and did a degree type other people weren't interested.

Note: I should mention when you apply for one of these more specialised degrees, if you don't get it then the university reconsiders your application for a normal degree. So in a way you're getting two chances to go to that university for one application. (At least in my experience)

Conclusion:

I want to wrap up this blog post by saying, you only get to go to university for a few years. I highly encourage you to make the most of it and that all starts with your degree choice. You might don't want to do a specialised degree, lots of universities don't offer these choices. But when you see one, consider it, learn about it, have fun with it.

If the degree aligns with what you want then

consider applying for it. It might be great, it might open doors, it might be life-changing.

But only you can make that decision.

And whatever you decide, I wish you the best of luck on your university journey.

WHAT IS CLEARING FOR UNIVERSITY STUDENTS?

Whilst there is hardly tons I can say in this introduction, I want to mention that whilst this isn't for everyone (including me). You never know if this might be useful in the future to you or a friend or a family member, so definitely check out this chapter because you never ever know when it might be needed.

<u>What is Clearing for University Students?</u>

Of all the different components of the university application process, there is always one part that confuses everyone, and at first, I was no exception. That part is clearing. In this blog post, we'll be exploring what clearing is and why it's useful?

<u>What is Clearing?</u>

In my experience, whilst the vast majority of university students won't need to worry about clearing. I think it's still important to have an awareness of it in case you do need it.

Therefore, clearing is how universities and other higher education establishments fill places on their courses that haven't been filled. They do this by allowing students to apply for courses that have spare spaces.

However, before you get too excited, you can only apply to clearing if you haven't already got a university place and/ or if you didn't get the grades or requirements to meet your university offer.

For example, if you got a university offer but they required you to get three As in your exams, but you could 1 A and 2 Bs instead. Meaning you didn't get your university offer then clearing allows you to apply for courses that still have spaces.

In other words, even though you didn't get your preferred choice at university, there is still a chance you could get to university via clearing.

Why Is This Useful For University Students?

I know I already touched on this in the last section but I do want to hammer this point home. Because it's so important and I remember once talking about clearing at a 6th Form college two years ago and when a girl heard there was a 'safety net' for her to get her into university. She was delighted.

And this is the great thing about clearing is because it does give students another chance to get into university.

Of course, I always encourage students to try their best at their exams so they can get into their preferred university and course. But there is always the safety net of Clearing. (At least in the United Kingdom)

<u>Requirements of Clearing:</u>

Now we know what clearing is and why it's good, let's talk about the requirements.

According to UCAS.com, a person can use clearing if:

- They're applying after 30th June for university
- They didn't receive any offers or none they wanted to accept
- The student didn't meet the requirements of the offer
- They've declined their preferred choice of university (or firm place as they call it)
- The student has paid the multiple choice application fee of £26.

As you can see this doesn't apply to a lot of students but it's very useful for the people who need it. As well as at the end of the day universities need to fill their spaces, so they get their money!

<u>Quick Note on Clearing:</u>

Another reason to try and avoid clearing if you can (by focusing on your exams) is because you don't particularly have a choice about the university you go to. For example, let's say you live in the Southwest of England and you really, really want to study biology. But the closest university that has a biology space is in the East Midlands. Then you're going to be in a difficult spot because you need to decide how much do you want to go to university?

Conclusion:

Overall, clearing is a great way for students to get into university if they didn't get the requirements of the offer. Also whilst a lot of students won't need it, there are a lot of advantages for students that do need clearing.

I hope you got something from today's blog post.

Have a great day!

IS ONLINE OR IN-PERSON UNIVERSITY RIGHT FOR YOU?

This is definitely what I meant when I was talking about the difficulty of putting these chapters into a perfectly logical order. Since some might argue this next chapter and the two afterwards should have gone in the second chapter.

But I firmly believe these next few online university posts are critical for the future of higher education. And as future or current university students this is certainly something to bear in mind.

<u>Is Online or In-Person University Right For You?</u>

Even as soon as a few years ago, a traditional or in-person university was the only serious way to go if you wanted to get a degree. But now with more online universities popping up on to the scene this creates more amazing opportunities for students to go to a university and get a degree. But which option is right for you?

What Do You Want Out of University?

Of course the normal, logical answer here is to say you want a degree in the subject you love, and yes that's a good answer. But university is so much more than a degree and that isn't some marketing pitch about university life.

It's the truth.

For example, university Is different for everyone and what the word university means is different to everyone too.

Some people think university is about studying hard, lots of reading and getting a qualification and only that. That's okay.

Others believe university is about getting independence, exploring yourself and who you are, partying and clubbing and making friends.

Then there's lots of other ideas in-between.

Personally, I think I'm sort of in the middle. I love psychology and what I do, I want to be successful and study hard. Yet my degree isn't my life, I'm still sociable, a person who loves to cook, see people and do more creative tasks.

Therefore, I still love studying and learning but I make sure it doesn't consume me.

Meaning when it came to choosing a university I needed something that provided me with both. A university that meant I could study very well AND I needed it to provide me with a lot of opportunities.

Turning this over to you, you need to decide what do you want from your university life and pick a university that helps you.

Such as if you want a partying university life (you don't have to) with lots of friends and socialising. Then an online university might not be for you.

Equally, if you want to get a degree that isn't location dependent then online might be a good option for you.

<u>What's Happening In Your Life?</u>

The only reason why I have an awareness of this next area is because I work as a student ambassador for my university so I know lots of students aren't under 22s.

In addition, when it comes to choosing your type of university you need to decide it based on what's happening in your life. Since lots of people get caught up with the idea of the traditional university experience and believe it's the only way to do it.

It isn't.

If I tapped into my creative side and other things I do, I could tell you millions of stories about that trapping people and all the ways how that *"There's only one way to do something"* thinking is deadly when it comes to careers. But that's beyond the scope of this blog post.

Therefore, I highly recommend you look at your life and think about what you can deal with.

For example, if you're an 18 year old without any concerns or pressures that make you NEED to be at home 24/7 then a traditional, in-person university might not be a problem for you.

However, if you had sick family members, you're a carer, have children or a full-time job that you can't give up. Then online university offers a lot more flexibility and could be better.

How Flexible Can You Be?

Building upon the last section, we need to talk about flexibility in more depth because it's the main difference between online and in-person universities. Since online universities tend to be a lot more flexible with timings because they don't have lectures or seminars at a set time to the best of my knowledge.

Making this option great if you have a 9 til 5 job with kids and you don't sit down until they go to bed. Then you go to do your reading and watch your lectures.

On the other hand, if you don't have a full time job and you want to go to a physical university then go for it. It's up to you.

A Note From Me:

I think it might be helpful for you to know why I chose an in-person university in case you can see something in my thinking process that you want to do yourself.

I've always been a very independent person and I love being able to do things myself. As well as I have survived by myself when my parents have been on holiday and romantic getaways. Thus, for me university was never about independence or improving I can live by myself to myself.

Instead I wanted to go to university to get the

"university experience" just so I could say I had done it, and I was fortunate enough for my parents to pay for my accommodation for my first year. I was extremely grateful!

Then my university time (and I'm mainly talking about my first time because my second year was during the pandemic) became more about learning, meeting new friends and growing as a person.

For example, I became part of the baking society and loved it, I became great friends with some of my flatmates and I tried to learn Italian. That was a mistake! I can't do languages, I joke with myself from time to time that I can't even do English sometimes because of my stuttering when it's bad!

But it was still great fun.

Overall, university for me was about exploring myself, having fun and growing as a person.

Conclusion:

This blog post covers a massive topic but even though this post is a lot longer than my guidelines, I really hope this was useful to you and it's gotten you thinking about some of the choices you might want to think about.

I wish you all the best with your university journey.

IS ONLINE LEARNING HERE TO STAY FOR UNIVERSITY STUDENTS?

As I'm writing this little introduction a few months after writing this chapter, I want to say that everything in this post is just as true now as it was when I originally wrote it.

I definitely believe that we have gotten to a point where we all realise the great benefits of having both in-person and online university, and everything else that is mentioned in this post.

Therefore, definitely keep reading to learn more about this great area of learning and its possible future.

Is Online Learning Here To Stay For University Students?

When I was asked to write a blog post on this topic, I was both excited and a bit concerned because from having read tens of different posts myself on technological shifts since the pandemic started, I know this can go in several directions. But I will try to limit myself here by focusing on university students and how online learning will continue to affect them for the foreseeable future. This will definitely be interesting!

Is Online Learning Here To Stay?

Of course!

I don't think that should surprise anyone and if any of you gasped or rolled your eyes at that, then hopefully you'll learn a bit more in this post.

Personally, I don't see a problem with online learning moving forward. Not only because I am always, always engaged in some type of online learning, as I'm always doing at least one online course (I'm doing three as I write this), but because learning will become more flexible, hybrid and better in the long term, in my opinion.

Those three ideas we'll focus on now.

Online Learning and Flexibility

One of the massive downsides of traditional learning is you have to be in a fixed location at a fixed time on a fixed date. Now most of the time that will not be a problem in the slightest but if you're sick, overwhelmed or dealing with something that can cause you to miss out on that learning.

Subsequently, on the flip side, if the lecturer is out sick or can't make it for one reason or another, then all those students miss out for no fault of theirs (or the lecturer's).

Therefore, what online learning allows is a bit of flexibility, because even before the pandemic most universities recorded lectures for revision purposes and for people who couldn't go. This was great for students because of the clear revision benefits but it meant students could also be slightly more flexible if they really needed it.

This has only increased because of the pandemic, the point where online learning meant mainstream.

Since with universities now focusing on online learning, it means students can be flexible in what, when and how they want to study. Which is better for everyone.

Overall, online learning will continue because it can allow staff, students and others greater flexibility to their already busy university life.

Leading us to our next point.

<u>Hybrid and Online Learning</u>

Thankfully with the pandemic finally receding (I hope), we are all starting to return to the lecture theatre and go back to university. So I wouldn't blame you for thinking online learning is done with completely, but quite the opposite is happening, because now we have the hybrid approach to learning.

Meaning from what friends have told me, the vast majority of their classes have been in-person, but some of them have been online.

Personally I think it's a brilliant option because it works great for the vast majority of people. Since for students, it still allows them to see other amazing people in-person, get the traditional university experience and get to ask questions in person to their lecturer.

Yet they still get to have the flexibility of online learning that they can fit into their schedule and plan around their assignment and coursework more effectively. As that was always one of the biggest pains about in-person teaching (and why lots of people didn't come towards the end of deadlines) because the in-person lecture was fixed, people skipped it so they could focus on their coursework.

At least some online learning is a workaround.

On the other hand for lecturers (which are important to remember because they're great people too!), they get to still see their students (which they do enjoy), they get to teach the topic they love and they still get the flexibility benefits of online learning if they need it.

Overall, online learning is here to stay because it offers a great hybrid option to learning that wasn't available before. As well as this hybrid option has many benefits for both students and lecturers alike.

Online Learning and The Long Term

Long time readers of this blog and The Psychology World Podcast, won't be surprised that I mentioned the long term here, because I always focus on it over the short term. Therefore, I have to mention it when we talk about online learning. Since online learning can be sustainable for the long term and it is arguably more resilient than traditional methods. For example, if the internet wasn't available during the global lockdowns, would we have been able to learn?

Almost certainly not. Or nowhere need as effectively as we did (and yes I am ignoring the educational inequalities that exist around the world in this case).

As a result, online learning can be beneficial for the long term success and sake of our learning due to that reason.

However, online learning also widens our opportunities for learning if you know where to look. For example, the tens (and probably hundreds in the future) of online courses I do always come from the same couple in the USA, and without online access to this knowledge, I would never be able to learn what I do. Therefore, in that regard, online learning has allowed me to access knowledge I never could have before.

In addition, if we step away from my personal example, we can see this growth in learning from places like online universities, online degrees and courses that allow people to upskill whilst fitting the learning in with their busy lives. This is a great advantage to full-time workers that still want to go to university, get a degree and improve their lives for the long term.

The Downside:

But of course, I am not blind to the fact that online learning has downsides. Yet as I've sprinkled throughout this blog post, traditional learning has downsides too. As well as there is a chance that these negatives will inhibit people's use and enjoyment of online learning.

For instance, the major problem of learning online was the loneliness that people experienced because of it. Since we couldn't see other people, have our casual (and normally funny) chats, we couldn't enjoy those strange little social moments like meeting someone for the first time amongst other things.

So of course, this must be managed. We must be careful that with online learning being here to stay, we still give ourselves, students and lecturers a chance to meet and socialise. You only have to look at the psychology literature to see how damaging lockdown in conjunction with online learning was to mental health.

Nonetheless, this is why I love the hybrid approach because you can still see people and it is the best of online and in-person learning joint together.

Then as a wider point and this is more for our own understanding, we must be mindful that not everyone has access to the same levels of technology as we do. For example, not everyone has access to their own laptop, computer or good broadband, and that is another downside to online learning that must be addressed.

And hopefully it will be in the future.

Conclusion:

I guess I sort of prelude to this in the opening of the post that it was going to be a bit longer than normal. But that is online learning... it is a great and powerful tool that really can transform lives for the better, if it is coupled with socialising and in-person learning. And whilst I will always continue to do various forms of online learning, I too will seek out in-person ones too because I want that connection and real-world learning.

So if you take anything away from this post, then please try and enjoy online learning because it is here to stay. That isn't something to be scared of, it is something to embrace because of the opportunities it gives us to flexibly learn, and counter. By making sure we engage with real-world people and in-person learning.

Online learning isn't going away, but when it gives us so many opportunities to learn. Why would you want it to?

WHAT IS ONLINE UNIVERSITY LIKE? TACKLING THE MYTHS

Myths.

As psychology students I definitely think that we know a lot more about myths than lots of other students from different disciplines. I'm not only talking about their underpinnings in cognitive and social psychology, but myths about us in particular.

For example, the stupid myths about psychology being a bad career option, we can analyse everything that something is saying and my personal favourite myth from all the old men, is mental health is just an excuse these days.

So as you can see as psychology students we know a lot about myths, but how does this apply to learning online?

<u>What is Online University Like? Tackling The Myths</u>

Whilst I write this towards the (hopeful) end of the COVID-19 Pandemic where students have spent the past 18 months learning online. I have no doubt online learning will continue in the future, especially with online degrees going more mainstream. In this blog post, you'll learn what it's actually like and what are some of the myths around online learning.

<u>What is Online University Like?</u>

I need to say upfront that this blog post is just my own personal experience and your experience is bound to be different. If only for the fact that when you hopefully attend online university, it's not in a pandemic!

Therefore, the way how my online university worked was you had all your lectures and seminars planned out ahead on your timetable. Then your readings and video lectures were sent out 48 hours before the scheduled lecture. Making the lecture a Q&A session.

Personally, I found this very good because online university meant we had more contact time with our lecturers compared to normal university. Meaning they were more available to us to answer questions and help us.

In addition, I much preferred the content being released 48 hours before the lecture because nothing was set in stone. Resulting in me being able to do the work when I wanted so it would fit around my life. Which is probably a lot better for students as it means they can plan relaxation time, going out with friends and other social activities. Making it better for your work/life balance.

Of course you need to make sure you still do the

work!

In terms of seminars and my practicals, they were done on Microsoft Teams and these were great because they gave us a chance to see other people, and get to know the other people on your course.

Leading us onto the myths.

<u>Myth: Online University is Isolating</u>

This was definitely one of my concerns and I think online university can be very isolating. But that's only if you let it be isolating because in my experience there were plenty of opportunities to see and meet people.

As I mentioned earlier, I saw and got to speak to plenty of people in my seminars and practical sessions because it was all on Teams. Even if your course doesn't offer Practical sessions, make sure you go to your seminars so you get to talk and interact with people. (And learn)

Another way how you can meet people is check out your university's societies (for the non-UK audience they're clubs or social groups that students run at university). During my second year at university, which was all online, I was the treasurer of my baking society. Therefore, most weeks I was on Teams, speaking to members of our groups, baking with them and I got to socialise a lot. To me that was great because it meant most weeks I had a guaranteed opportunity to have proper interactions with other people, and that's precious during a pandemic!

Overall, when you're doing Online University, it

doesn't have to be isolating and there are plenty of great ways to meet other people and talk to them.

Myth: Online University is Easier Than in Person University

I was shocked when I heard some students say this but some people honestly believe Online University is easier. My thoughts have always been: *what do you mean easier?*

Of course some people are going to mean it's easier to fit into your life, look after family, have a job, etc. and I completely agree in that regard Online University is easier than Traditional or in-person university.

However, if you believe Online University requires less work than in-person university, I'm sorry to say that that isn't how it works. Due to with Online University you still need to do the readings, watch the lectures, make notes and do the coursework.

Just because the university is online doesn't make them happy to accept subpar work, late assignments and students that don't want to do the work.

As I mentioned in the beginning of the post, I still had to do readings and watch lectures to make my notes. I still had to attend seminars and practical sessions for my degree.

Overall, if you want to go to university, be it in-person or online-only, then you still need to love the subject and have the work ethic.

Conclusion:

I hope you learnt something about online university and whilst I can't promise you you'll have the same experience. I loved in-person and online university and both were great experiences for me. As well as I hope I've cleared up some of the myths around it for you.

Good luck on your university journey.

HOW DOES UNIVERSITY ACCOMMODATION WORK FOR UNIVERSITY STUDENTS?

Accommodation at university is definitely one of the most important areas of university life to understand before you go to university. There are so many different to explore, have fun with and enjoy that I'm just going to dive into the post.

But remember that your accommodation option can basically determine your university life for the next year to some extent.

Enjoy!

How Does University Accommodation Work For University Students?

If you decided to go to a university that is far away from your home or far enough away that it makes more sense to pay for university accommodation, there are always questions about how it works. Since some people know how the accommodation works but lots of people don't, so they want an easy to understand guide that introduces them to the topic. Whilst this varies between different countries and different universities, I want to explain how (in my experience) university accommodation works in the UK.

How Does University Accommodation Work?

For the purposes of this post, we're going to be talking about on-campus accommodation or accommodation that is associated with the university, or dorm rooms for Americans. As well as I will probably explain the different accommodation options in another post.

Therefore, after you have confirmed your place at a university, you will be offered a chance to apply for university accommodation and you have to pick what accommodation you want. At most universities there is a wide range fitting an equally wide range of budgets and desires to choose from.

For example, at my university, you have the low budget shared bathroom, less good looking flat options up to the en-suite and shared kitchen very nice flats.

So when it comes to you choosing what you want to apply for, it's important to ask yourself:

- What can you afford?
- What do you want?
- Can you see yourself enjoy being there for the year?

Also I the reason why I mentioned the *what do you want* point is because I wasn't going to live somewhere with a shared bathroom with strangers for a year. That just wasn't happening. And yes I know I sound like a complete snob, but we all have our red lines.

Anyway, you'll apply for your accommodation through the university's website and I won't go too much into that because it's different for each university. As well as I applied three years ago so I don't remember it too much.

In addition, I will say that a lot of university accommodation is reserved for first year students with a small selection being open to applications from later year students. Which I say I unofficially recommend if you can, do stay on campus or in university accommodation in your first year. Mainly for the sake of just experiencing what it's like.

Sure I didn't like some of it and I've always been extremely independent.

But I know for lots and lots of students, they benefit greatly from being away from home. Yet everyone is different in different situations and circumstances so that is just food for thought.

After you've sent off your application, it will be accepted or rejected.

If it's rejected I think you might be offered a second choice if you picked one. Or you'll have to make other arrangements.

If it's accepted then you effectively sign the lease and set up the payment schedule. From what I remember you pay the accommodation fees in rough thirds at the beginning of each term.

Other Tips:

I realise that this post is a little shorter than usual but I want to make it is useful to you so I want to add a few extra accommodation tips.

Firstly, it goes without saying but I have seen plenty of students fall into this trap. Pick what you can afford, you will be at university in your first year having readings, lectures and assignments to do. You do not need any extra stress or concern on your shoulders, so do not get a place you can't afford. Otherwise you will be panicking and constantly worrying about how you're going to pay for the accommodation.

Secondly, from what I remember all my university accommodation options included utilities so if you can find that I would suggest you take that option. Since it meant I didn't have to pay for tons of extras.

Finally, university accommodation is definitely an experience, and if you've listened to my podcast or read any of my other posts, then you know I am not a partying or clubbing person. But I still really enjoyed the accommodation experience because you get to meet some amazing people, learn great things about yourself and others and... for me living at university is all a part of the experience.

So if you can, you might want to check it out.

If for no other reason than you can say you've done it, and you won't forever be wondering if you've missed out on something in later life.

WHAT ARE YOUR ACCOMMODATION OPTIONS AT UNIVERSITY?

To finish up this little section on accommodation options and this is the penultimate chapter in this section of the book, we need to talk specifically about the different accommodation options. Since these can affect your possible commute, social life and other aspects of your university life for the next year.

So read on and just remember that university is about doing what you want and having fun. If that means you wanting to live at home that's perfectly fine. No matter what other people tell you.

What Are Your Accommodation Options At University?

Continuing with our look at accommodation for university students, I want to take a broader look at the options you have, because university accommodation isn't your only option and some people can't afford it. Therefore, the entire point of this post is to explain what your other options are so you have the foundation knowledge to start investigating for yourself.

<u>University Accommodation:</u>

In the last post, I explained how this type of accommodation university works and there are great advantages to it. For example, if you go to a campus university (or a city university for that matter) then you're closer to all the major facilities, saving you money on travelling potentially, you get to experience university life more often and it's another way to make friends.

Additionally, one of my favourite benefits is probably how university accommodation tends to include all your utilities in the cost, meaning no extras. As well as lots of students love the independence it gives them as they're living away from home.

Also it is worth noting that in the grand scheme of things, university accommodation is only really practical for first year students as the majority of accommodation is reserved for their use. Yet some universities, like mine, do have some accommodation blocks available for returning students after first year, so research what your university does if you're interested in that.

However, the main downside of university accommodation is depending on the university, even the most affordable accommodation can be… rubbish, and the more liveable accommodation can be extremely expensive.

Then again, my university had some great

accommodation at good prices, but I remember from my university open days at different universities, some accommodation was lacking for the price!

All in all, when it comes to looking at university accommodation, think about what you want, what you can afford and if you're going to be happy there for the year.

<u>University Students Living In Private Accommodation:</u>

Whilst I have had no experience with this option personally, I do have a lot of friends who have done this option.

Therefore, after your first year of university, you might want to start looking for private accommodation to rent for the following academic year. There are plenty of websites to find these options and if you do a google search, talk to other students or look at your university's website then you should be able to find some.

Then after you've found an affordable choice, it's a matter of signing the lease and sorting out all of that stuff.

However, accommodation costs can be very expensive in private accommodation and it doesn't always include utilities (like water, internet and other costs). Which is why the vast majority of students house share and live with friends. It's a great money saving idea as you all pitch in to pay the rent and the other bills equally, making it more affordable than living alone.

Granted you need to find friends you actually want to live with!

Furthermore, the only other downside of private accommodation that springs to mind is the length of the lease as the length of university accommodation is the academic year. This runs from September to mid-to-late June. Meaning you only need to pay for those months but the disadvantage of private accommodation in my opinion is you need to pay for the full twelve months.

Which isn't good if you plan to move back home after the end of June because you'll no longer be at university.

That's just something to think about.

But as I said earlier, I have no experience of this set up so please do your own investigating too.

<u>Living At Home</u>

Of course this depends on your own family, family and personal circumstances and more, but we're going to take a broad look at living at home and commuting to university.

If you live relatively close to your university then you could commute to university each day and live at home.

Personally I love this idea because I've been doing it for the past two years. As I know it's a lot cheaper than living in private or university accommodation as I don't have to pay rent (And even if I did, we've all said it would be a lot less than "real" rent).

Another benefit is I get to see my family a lot more and I get to stay in the loop with everything. As well as living at home means I get everything I need in my room anyway and there's no risk of me forgetting to take something and not being able to get it for a while.

Of course, there are some disadvantages. For example, even though I only live 30 minutes away by car from the university. I can't (technically) drive yet so it involves a half an hour walk to the train station, a 45-minute train journey depending on the day and time then another 30-minute walk to the university.

However, the train costs is still a lot lower than any sort of rent and I do enjoy walking so I hardly mind.

As well as something I want to remind everyone of is it is very unlikely you are going to be at university for five days a week. Meaning you will probably only need to pay for the train (or whatever transportation you use) for a few days a week. Personally, I think that is a lot better than paying 7 days of rent every single day.

Overall, this accommodation option is very dependent on your own circumstances and what you want. I know some students just find it easier to live at university and not at home. I completely understand that and it really is down to you.

Conclusion:

Accommodation at university is a topic that lots of students who are thinking of going to university get concerned about, as they don't understand at first. Therefore, I hope, if any, this post has helped you to realise the wide range of possible options for you in your first and following years at university.

Whatever you decide remember you need to do what is right for you and your circumstances, and I wish you the best of luck.

ARE SCHOLARSHIPS A GOOD IDEA FOR UNIVERSITY STUDENTS?

I definitely wish that this was an area that students and schools focused on more before people went to university. Since students can get a lot of money in scholarships in some situations if they look for them, apply and ultimately get accepted.

Personally I love scholarships and bursaries so I feel like this is a critical chapter that you definitely need to read and might make your university life a bit easier. At least on the potential finance side.

Are Scholarships A Good Idea For University Students?

Scholarships at university seem to be a strange area of the university experience, because it seems to be mystical and filled with myths that put students off them. Personally I love them and in this blog post I'll be dispelling of the myths and giving you a few unofficial hints about how to find them.

What Are Scholarships At University?

Simply put, scholarships are schemes designed by the university to give certain people something that benefits them in exchange for something that benefits the university.

Well, that was as clear as mud.

A better explanation would be through my university I have the Student Ambassador Scholarship meaning the university gives me £1,000 ($1,500) per academic year for the course of my degree in exchange for me working 200 hours for them where I represent them and help out at events.

There are more benefits to me than just the money, but personally that is what I focus on.

Therefore, as you can see, scholarships are generally great because they help you as much, if not more than the university itself. So it is a win-win for everyone.

In addition, universities have a wide range of scholarships for different people. For example, I seem to remember a lot of sport scholarships at my university (I was never going to apply for them!), academic-based ones for the brightest students and then there were scholarships for ethnic minority students.

Personally my biggest tip when it comes to universities and scholarships is, make sure you look at what your university offers. I'm really glad that I looked at the Student Ambassador one because I get a good amount of money, I get to meet and work with great people and I get a lot of other skills that I wouldn't get otherwise.

So definitely look at them when you have made your choices about universities.

Also I should add that the great thing about scholarships is the money are loans. They're grants instead. Meaning that money is yours and you don't need to repay it.

What Are The Downsides Of Scholarships?

As always I like to give you the full picture when it comes to university so we need to talk about the downsides of scholarships. Since I know that is what some of you are wondering.

And to be honest, there are no downsides.

I've had my Student Ambassador scholarship for three years now, even though it's on pause whilst I'm on my placement, and there isn't a single thing I can complain about (and before you ask, no I'm not hiding anything out of fear of losing my scholarship). Sure there has been the odd moment of stress and lots of funny stories, but nothing bad.

Then I have spoken to other people too with different scholarships and they have nothing to complain about either.

So the real question is simple: are there any downsides to applying?

No!

It might take you a bit of time to fill out the application form and do whatever is needed for the application process. But the only thing stopping you from applying and taking a chance is you.

When I applied for my student ambassador scholarship, I was nervous, concerned and I even missed the first interview, because I got lost walking from the train station. I think I ended up in some remote village on the outskirt of Canterbury.

My point is, you need to try. You need to apply for some scholarships because you never know what will happen and what it will give you.

Take it from me. Scholarships are worth it.

How To Find University Scholarships?

As scholarships can be great attractions for certain types of students, universities tend to make it easy to find. Therefore, if you just look on the university website you should be able to find them. As well as a quick google search of "INSERT UNIVERSITY NAME scholarships" that should bring up what you're looking for.

Conclusion:

After looking at all of this, are scholarships a good idea for university students?

Yes.

Not only because of the extra money the scholarship might give you, but because of the extra opportunities it might provide. You might get to meet amazing new people, learn new valuable skills and do things you never knew happened.

But you need to part yourself out there and enjoy looking for them. Scholarships aren't hard to find, and yes some of them will not be right for you, but others might be. So please, have a look, apply for some and just see where they take you.

You never know, you might be pleasantly surprised.

PART TWO: DURING UNIVERSITY

HOW TO PICK OPTIONAL MODULES AT UNIVERSITY?

Whilst I completely admit this next section of the book is rather short compared to the first and last of the book. It is absolutely no less critical because these next two topics will definitely pop up in your mind at least once or twice during your university years, and then you will certainly be pleased you have read them.

And even if don't end up thinking about the topics in these two chapters, then your friends definitely will. So these next chapters (and the entire book to be completely honest with you) might help you be a better friend in the long term as you'll know exactly to do or say. Well that's the idea anyway.

As well as this first chapter on picking optional module is just brilliant, and you'll definitely understand why I love optional modules by the end of the post.

Enjoy!

How To Pick Optional Modules At University?

Some degrees allow you to pick optional modules as a part of your degree, and these are brilliant for students for various reasons. However, some students struggle to figure out how to pick them or are nervous about taking the freedom that they can provide you with. Therefore, the point of this blog post is to help you understand what they are, why they're great and how to pick optional modules. This is going to be great fun!

What Are Optional Modules?

In your degree, you will always have compulsory modules that will form the backbone of your degree, for lack of a better term, but sometimes you won't have enough modules to make up the credits (you don't need to worry about these) you need for that year. Resulting in you having to take optional modules to get the rest of your credits.

For example, in my first year of university, my compulsory modules took up all of my credits except enough credits for one extra module, so I needed to take one optional module to make up my credits.

On the other hand, some years in your degree you might not have any optional modules. This is especially true if your degree needs to be accredited (approved) by a professional body.

For example, in psychology, our accrediting body requires us to be taught certain topics so we have a large breadth and depth of understanding. Now, most of this compulsory teaching happens in second year so I didn't have any optional modules that year.

All in all, optional modules are modules you get to choose what the topic is and then you take these on top of your compulsory modules.

<u>Why Are Optional Modules Great?</u>

Sometimes I think optional modules are better than compulsory ones, because optional modules are great as they give you the ability to explore whatever you want and they allow you to tailor your degree to your interests to some extent.

For example, my degree is psychology with clinical psychology (mental health), so my degree naturally skews in one direction because I wanted the more specialise undergraduate degree.

However, this meant I couldn't explore beyond that too much. Yet optional modules allowed me to explore forensic psychology as part of my degree because I was really interested in that, but my degree didn't explicitly allow exploration of that.

<u>How To Pick Them?</u>

Building upon the last section, we're now moving onto the area that puzzles or confuses a lot of students because they either don't want to take advantage of the freedom that optional modules give you or they're don't know how to.

Additionally, what I mean by freedom in terms of optional modules is simple. Within reason you can pick any optional module you want from any topic, subject or degree.

I will mention that there isn't complete freedom

because some modules are prerequisites and other modules will clash with your compulsory ones, so you can't take them. But you will find plenty of modules that you can pick.

Leading us to the question of, how do you pick them?

I really think this all comes down to you as a person and what you want from university. So for the sake of ease, I'm going to tell you my ways of thinking about optional modules and I'm quite glad I had optional modules in my first and final year because I've used both thinking processes.

Firstly, you could just pick other topics within your degree that you find interesting. This is what almost everyone does and I did this in my first year, as I choose forensic psychology. Not only is this a great way to explore your degree subject in more depth and expand your knowledge, but you might find a new passionate area for yourself in the process.

That happened to me with forensic psychology.

Secondly, you would use university and its education to explore passionate areas or interests you have that have nothing to do with your degree.

For instance, I work as a Student Ambassador, and my mentor used optional modules to customise her degree into a philosophy degree. Therefore, whilst philosophy had nothing to do with her "proper" degree, she still took advantage of these modules to explore an interest she had.

You can do the same if you want.

For me, I have seriously looked into accounting, tax, company law and some other modules at university but the only modules I have found that match what I want are either for first years (not third years) or they have prerequisites that I don't have.

Then again, I have found an optional module that is akin to Entertainment Law that a person I have a working relationship with in America is doing at the moment.

Therefore, I might try that in addition to the other psychology optional modules I'll be choosing.

The point of this section is to say, at the end of the day, it is your degree and you need to do what is right for you.

Conclusion:

As I mentioned in the paragraph above, you need to do what is right for you. You might hate the idea of exploring topics outside of your degree, that's fine. It's might excite you to explore things outside of your degree subject, that's fine too.

For me, it feels right to explore certain topics outside of psychology, but it doesn't mean it's right for you.

If anything, the entire point of this blog post has been awareness. Awareness is critical in all aspects of life, but especially when it comes to university so we can make the most of this time in our lives.

I still think optional modules are great, and whatever optional modules you decide on picking I hope you have fun and enjoy them.

Just remember, to make the most of your university time in both the social and learning aspects.

SHOULD I CHANGE MY DEGREE AT UNIVERSITY?

To wrap up this little section, I wanted to leave you with this thought-provoking chapter on changing your degree. Why you should, shouldn't and might want to think about it.

Just in case.

Should I Change My Degree At University?

Whilst we will all experience some kind of self-doubt at university and whether we have chosen the right degree at times. Then we learnt we made the right choice and stick to it, for some people they do need to change their degrees. In this blog post, I'll help you to understand why you should or shouldn't change your degree at university.

Why Shouldn't You Change Your Degree?

This first point really links back to the point about self-doubt. We all experience it when it comes to university and sometimes that can cause us to think about changing our degrees. For example, in my first two weeks at university and we were covering the introductory things to psychology, I started to wonder about it myself. I was wondering if psychology was still right for me, should I change it or just give up all together.

That's a classic example of self-doubt and to be honest, everyone will experience that at some point.

Then I experienced self-doubt again after my first group project and along some other parts of the degree. I really wasn't sure if I wanted to continue with my degree. Mainly because of my minor inability to write academically or as academically as the university would like me too.

I'm telling you this so you never feel alone in what you're thinking and I want you to know what is normal to experience at university.

You might want to check out this post to help you with your self-doubt. How To Overcome Imposter Syndrome?

However, I stuck it out. Things improved and I'm extremely happy that I didn't change my degree.

Therefore, that is definitely something you need to consider. Sometimes you really do just need to hang it out, talk to people and things will improve.

Yet if things don't, go and talk to your school at university and see if they can help you. Then after that conversation and others with your friends, then consider about changing your degree.

It is rare you'll actually want to, but sometimes it is needed.

Why Should You Change Your Degree?

Before I apply the reasons to you, I want to tell you about an older friend of mine because she changed her degree and never regretted it. What happened was she went to the University of Oxford in the 90s to study Classic Arabic, went in the classroom in the first day and the teacher got them to speak ancient Arabic words he had written up on the board. She didn't know a single one of them.

So she went to her head of college (because Oxford is divided up into Colleges not schools), asked what else the college had on offer and she was told to write an essay on theology (you wouldn't need to do that unless you there) and they'll see what happened. Then she completed a degree in theology.

How Does This Apply To You?

I wanted to tell you about that real-life example because it shows one reason why you might want to change your degree. Because whilst the first year of university is almost like a step down from High or Secondary school education (or whatever your country's equivalent is). If you encounter a subject that you really wanted to explore but it turns out you know absolutely nothing about it.

Then maybe a change is in order.

Then again, maybe you'll pick up the subject in time.

However, that example also shows that changing your degree isn't a sign of failure in the slightest. Sometimes you need to make a change so you can thrive.

In addition, maybe you should change your degree if you realise you don't love it anymore. I have spoken about this many times on the blog, because you need to love your degree subject to drive you through the difficult times. For example, my love for psychology helps me through the assessments and general university aspects that I hate.

Therefore, if you don't love your subject anymore then maybe you need to change it to something else that you do love.

I remember back when I was in sixth form (16-18 year old education) and there was a girl in my class that wanted to do veterinary science and another thing related to biology. I think she went for veterinary science in the end, but if it turned out she didn't like it, she could always switch over to the other one.

The Most Important Factor In Should I Change My Degree?

Finally, the massive reason why you might want to change your degree is simple, what is best for you?

It is perfectly all well and good me writing about my thoughts and opinions on changing your degree. But at the end of the day, you need to take a step back and inspect your life to see what you truly want. You need to consider your mental health, your future, your happiness and everything that impacts this decision.

And as always I never say things to scare you. I

say these things to make you focus on this decision because once you make it, it can be rather difficult to change or revert back. So please think long and hard about your decision.

Sometimes you will need to change your degree for your sake.

Sometimes (most of the time) you won't.

I'm really glad that I hang out on my degree and didn't decide to change it, because I'm learning, doing what I love and my degree has given me a lot of great opportunities that other degrees wouldn't give me. Like my placement, the great people and projects I'm currently working on.

Just remember. Do what is right for you and your future, and you'll be fine.

PART THREE: THIRD YEAR AND BEYOND

EXPECTATION SETTING FOR FINAL YEAR MODULES

For the final section of this book, I wanted to talk about the third year of university specifically because it is important. Especially this next chapter because I was very shocked about this and I really, really don't want any of you to suffer the same disappointment as me.

<u>Expectation Setting For Final Year Modules</u>

When it comes to your final year at university, lots of students have the option to choose some of their own modules. This allows you to customise your degree more towards your own interests, but as I write this, I have just finished choosing my modules and there were plenty of things I would have liked to know beforehand. Therefore, in this blog post, I'll talk about my own experience and give you some advice so you can hopefully avoid my "mistakes".

Why Should You Think About Your Modules Earlier?

Throughout your second year at university (or whatever the year before your final year is called), it's a great idea to look into what modules your university allows you to take next year. This means if there are plenty of choices for you, then it gives you a bit of extra time to decide the direction you want your final year to go in.

Additionally, thinking about it earlier allows you to weigh up what factors are important to you, and so you can find modules that meet those requirements. That bit can be slightly time consuming. For example, if you're better at coursework then you might want to choose modules that are more coursework focused.

How Does Choosing Your Final Year Modules Works: The Perception

Of course, everything in these blog posts are just my own opinions, thoughts and experiences. But I really don't see why any university would be different from these major points in this post.

Therefore, I fully believed when it came to choosing my optional modules for my final year. I would be given basically free rein to choose what I wanted because it was my degree and I wanted to learn about what I was interested in.

Also I thought I would be free to pick modules from almost any other school outside the School of Psychology.

Now I can almost feel some of you readers start

to sink a little as you might have realised where I'm going with this post. Some of you might have thought about doing a module you would never do normally, others might have wondered about trying a module in a different subject area in case you wanted to do a postgraduate degree in a completely different area to your bachelor's, and the rest of you might not have thought about this at all.

I don't blame you!

How Does Choosing Your Final Year Modules Works: The Reality

However, the reality is a lot more strict than I realised. Since I knew that I would have to follow my requirements set up by my psychology degree. I interpreted that as me having to do my four compulsory modules and I would have free rein on the last two.

Yet this was far from the case, because of two main reasons.

Firstly, I love copyright law and learning about the legal side of the entertainment industry. From copyright in regards to books to the entertainment law about Hollywood and other things. Mainly because an American friend of mine is doing a course in this at her university and whenever she spoke about it, I was really, really interested in the subject matter.

Therefore, when I discovered I was only able to choose certain modules within psychology, and very few outside of the school. I was a bit disappointed and that was why I wanted to do this post, so you understood that you cannot just choose your modules too freely.

Sorry if I've shocked some people. It's better that you know now about this and not get disappointed when it comes to choosing your modules.

Secondly… well that requires a tip-full section below.

Make Sure You Read Your Requirement Like A Textbook For An Exam

Granted that headline is a bit long for my liking but it is true. I have had to exchange a good amount (2) emails with the university staff in charge of sorting out final year modules, because of the requirements.

Since your modules will (might?) be divided into two groups. Group 1 as it was told to us was the more theoretical modules then Group 2 were the practical modules.

Personally I think that sounds really, really easy, because I have two optional modules left and my degree requires I choose one from each group. I should just do that shouldn't I?

Well no, because when it comes to registering interest in these modules for my final year online, there are no groups like that. Instead you have to pick from some slightly changed groups and then you're done.

Tips:

My biggest tip for you is to make sure you read your degree requirements when picking your modules. This you can easily find on your university website and you'll probably be emailed it again when it comes to choosing your modules.

However, I cannot stress enough just look at the groups within those requirements and you'll be fine. As well as I know not all of this makes perfect sense right now, but I promise you when it comes to choosing your modules. You will definitely be grateful for this little blog post and hopefully you'll remember some of this advice.

Personally, if I had read the degree requirements in the handbook instead of reading the other stuff the university emailed me. I definitely wouldn't have had this much trouble choosing my two optional modules. Since apparently I kept choosing modules that I was really interested in, but because the groups they were in weren't compatible with the degree requirements. I had to choose new ones.

Spare yourself that pain! Read your degree requirement in your course handbook!

What about one last tip?

In my opinion, I wouldn't really call this a tip but more of a common sense thing that gets overlooked. Just make sure the modules you pick don't give you more modules in one university term compared to the other.

For example, my compulsory modules were 2 in the Autumn term, 2 in the spring term. But because I was really interested in my first two optional modules, I didn't even think about checking what term they were in, so they were both in the spring term. Meaning I had 2 modules in the Autumn term, 4 in the Spring term.

Leading to some emails and that was why I had to choose new modules in the first place.

Therefore, make sure you check when your modules are in the university year and don't overload yourself, because you will have to change it.

Conclusion:

As always none of these blog posts are ever, ever meant to be negative. As well as the point of this post was just to get you to realise the reality of choosing modules, and making sure you avoid some of the minor pitfalls that I haven't.

And to be honest, choosing your final year modules is hardly a negative experience, it can actually be a lot of fun and get you excited for the next academic year and your future after that.

WHAT TO DO AFTER UNIVERSITY?

The topic of this next chapter is sort of one of those horrible but very much needed questions that pops up in every university student's mind. As well as I can tell you from personal experience that it does change, so even if you're a brand new university student who thinks they know exactly what they're doing after their undergraduate degree.

Please change your mindset slightly now to at least be open to the possibility of that not working out or you wanting to change your mind.

It is natural and a very, very real possibility.

But that could be both a bad thing, or an extremely positive thing!

<u>What To Do After University?</u>

What to do after university? Is a major question on the mind of most students. Especially if you're entering the final year of your bachelor's degree, so the aim of this post is to help make you aware of some of the options available to you. Not only does this allow you to start planning your future, but they'll be some questions too so you can find out if this choice is right for you.

Why Do You Need To Think About What To Do After University?

The most important reason to do this is because some of these options need you to do things in your final year. Therefore, if you know what you're aiming for after your degree, you can start to prepare and position yourself for this in the final year. For example, if you want a job after your degree, then looking at how to improve your employability is important.

Speaking of which.

Getting A Job:

After working for three (or however long your degree is) years, you might decide that you don't want to study for a Masters or PhD and instead you want to get a job. There is nothing wrong with this and the vast majority of students do this option.

Whether you get a job in your degree subject or in another sector entirely that is down to you. But because you have a degree, as far as employers are concerned, you are clever and you have a lot of transferable skills that might be useful to them. For example, critical thinking, analysis and evaluation skills would be useful to a very wide range of businesses.

In addition, even if you realise in your final year (or at any point for that matter) that you don't want to work in your degree subject area. Don't despair because your degree has still taught you a lot of valuable skills that employers want.

However, the only thing I would say against this option is where do you want to work?

Due to if you want to work in a science field then this option is not for you, technically. For example, if I wanted a psychology job then I would have to move onto a Masters and then probably a PhD to get a good psychology job. It's just one of the good things about the psychology job market.

Meaning if you want a job that requires a lot of education, this option isn't available to you. Unless you want to take a break from education then return to it so you can get your dream job.

Overall, getting a job and leaving education is a great option to consider.

Ascend To Higher Education:

Technically, you're already in higher education but we'll skip over that little detail (it should be higher-higher education).

However, if you don't want to get a job after finishing university, you could continue your education if your life allows it. As well as there will be future blog posts on the benefits and how do Masters and PhDs work.

Personally, this is the option I'll take because after my psychology degree. I'm intending to do a clinical psychology (mental health) Masters so I can continue my education. As well as whilst I might not do a PhD, there are still plenty of psychology jobs available with a Masters.

And this is what you need to consider when deciding what you want to do. You need to decide what will help you most and what will you enjoy. For instance, getting an everyday job outside psychology, I won't enjoy and by doing a Masters this will help me get the jobs I'm more likely to enjoy. As well as choose as a career.

On the whole, if you want or need to continue with your education so you can get the job you want in the future. Then doing a Masters, PhD or whatever your subject calls it (I know Law and accounting have some weird titles) can be a great idea.

<u>Cannot Decide:</u>

I know plenty of people who just cannot decide what they want to do after their degree. They don't know if they should get a job, continue with another degree or do something else entirely. Sometimes this is scary to them because they feel like they should know, because surely everyone knows.

So if this is you, then you aren't alone in these feelings.

Therefore, I would say what I've said in numbers of blog posts. Focus on the long term and what you want to achieve (also known as goals), and if you don't know what you want to achieve, then sort that out first.

Once you know what you want for the long term, it will start to help you understand what you need to get there.

For instance, if you wanted to be an academic in, let's say, microbiology. Then you can start to think about what you need to do to achieve it. Like getting a Masters, PhD and getting research experience.

It's something to think about and of course these goals and long term focuses change. I think I've changed mine ten times since starting to think about psychology, but I know what I want to achieve now.

Overall, if you can't decide what you want, then look at your goals and go from there.

Conclusion:

As I (and thousands of other students) start my final year in September, I know lots of people will be scared by this topic. But hopefully after reading this blog post, you'll start to have some awareness about the options available to you after you leave university.

Finishing university doesn't have to be a step into the darkness and unknown. It just has to be something you'll enjoy and want to do for years to come.

And that's critical.

Because once you lose the enjoyment and fun in something, what's the point of doing it for another few decades?

There isn't.

Just bear that in mind and you'll be fine.

WHY DO A MASTERS DEGREE?

Over the course of the next four chapters, we're going to look at some options of what you could do after you finish university, well the undergraduate stage of university at least.

Personally, I think these are some rather critical to read chapters because these really do give a lot of breath and depth into possible options you can do after university. And as I mention in the introductions for these chapters, you start to get an understanding of how difficult it is to find easy to understand and simply information about these options.

Basically, I would have loved to these chapters at an early stage of my university journey.

I hope they help you and maybe even inspire you a little.

Why do A Masters Degree?

With me starting my final year at university in a few months, I wanted (and needed) to start thinking about what I wanted to do after I graduate. I know

I've covered *What To Do After University?* In another blog post, but now I wanted to focus on doing a Masters Degree specifically. Yet in case you're unsure whether this is a good thing or not for you, I'll explain the benefits, the drawbacks and my own thinking process towards a Masters Degree.

What Is A Masters Degree?

Just so everyone is on the same page, a Masters Degree is the type of degree you do after a bachelors but before a PhD, and yes I know that was extremely oversimplified. But that's the simplest definition of what it is, and I'll be defining a Masters Degree through the post as its benefits are rather unique compared to a Bachelor's.

However, just like a Bachelor's you can do a Masters of the Arts or Sciences, with Masters of Sciences focusing on scientific research, rigour and methods.

What Are The Benefits of Doing a Masters?

More Specialisation:

This is definitely one of the greatest benefits in my opinion about doing a Masters. Since they allow you to specialise in your degree subject and become more of an expert in that little (or large) area.

Then this specialised knowledge can be very useful in allowing you to get access to even higher levels of education and it allows you to become a lot better in a specialised area.

For example, at the moment, I study psychology as a Bachelors. Therefore, in a way, I know a lot of topics within psychology at a good amount of depth, so I have a good breathe and depth of knowledge.

However, a masters degree would allow me to deep dive into clinical psychology (just think mental health) and really focus on that fascinating area. Allowing me to become a lot more knowledgeable about a very wide range of topics within that area.

Personally, I really like the sound of that because I am passionate about that subfield and I do want to learn more.

Therefore, if there's an area of your degree subject that you want to explore and increase your expertise in. Then a Master's degree might be a great idea for you.

Access To Higher Paying Jobs:

Now this is a major reason why I want to do a Masters, because one of the reasons why I chose to do a psychology degree (besides from how interesting it was), was because you cannot do anything in the psychology job market without a Masters degree at the least.

Now I know that might scare, concern or worry some people, but I like it. Since it means you'll only be competing against other degree educated people (at least that's the lie I tell myself to pretend getting a job will be easier).

Therefore, there are plenty of job markets, especially in the sciences, that require you to have an advanced degree before they will even consider your job application. As a result, if you want to work in one of these fields then this is a very good reason to consider doing a Masters.

As well as even if you do want to work in a sector that doesn't require you to have a degree. It could still be a good idea because it might give you an extra leg up in the job application process, but that depends on the employers and whatever job you go for.

Drawbacks To Doing A Masters:

However, as much as I love the idea of doing a Masters. I suppose I better try to keep this balanced, so here are the potential downsides of doing a Masters degree.

Another Year Out of Work:

Personally I didn't know this was a reason against it, because I believed students would actually see that as a benefit. But it turns out lots of people see this very much as a negative, so we need to explore this drawback.

After talking to different people over the past few months, I realise that this drawback comes down to a few different things.

Firstly, people are concerned that after spending the past three or four (or however long your degree is) years at university. They might be better off starting work, increasing their employability and getting out into the real world.

Personally, I do completely understand that. But as I said before a Masters degree could make you even more employable depending on your desired job, and you can still increase your employability whilst studying. That's what part-time jobs are for.

Secondly, people are concerned about the cost, the debt, etc. Which I'll address below, but if you're living in the UK then it very arguable that the maintenance and tuition fee loans are basically free money. But I cannot comment on how it works for other countries, especially the US.

Finally, without realising it, they're lying to themselves that they want to continue in education. I have seen this a fair amount of times where people are telling me they want to do a masters but X, Y and Z are stopping them. Then after a while, I manage to get it out of them that they don't really want to do another degree.

And that's fine.

There is absolutely nothing wrong with just having a bachelors degree. That's still amazing.

Yet I know there are normally family, personal or other reasons why people don't like to admit that they don't want to continue, and I'm afraid that is something you definitely need to deal with yourself. There's no advice whatsoever I can offer there to help you.

<u>Cost:</u>

I'm actually really glad I did this blog post because there's a very strong myth going around universities that you only get 4 years of government funding in the UK. But I just did a bit of research and thankfully UK students can apply for postgraduate funding, so that's thankfully no longer a factor for me.

Anyway, I do know that not all students have those luxuries, especially amongst our international audience (Granted some non-UK students have to pay a few hundred, not thousands of their currency for their degree. I wish that was an option here).

Therefore, if you are concerned about the cost of a Masters or another type of postgraduate study. Then I would unofficially recommend you look at possible scholarships, bursaries and loans that might be able to help you out.

I know that money and the cost of university is never an easy topic, but it is still a factor we must all consider.

Conclusion:

I'm really looking forward to the idea of doing a Masters degree, because I do want to become specialised in clinical psychology and deepen my knowledge on the subject. As well as I do want to be able to possibly go after those higher-paying jobs.

However, I know not everyone wants that, especially when we consider it's another year out of work and the cost of the degree itself, and that's fine. You don't need to have a postgraduate degree.

Just think about your options, what's right for you and your situation, and you should be fine.

At the end of the day, just do what makes you happy.

HOW DO MASTERS DEGREES WORK?

Now we all understand why you might want to do a Masters degree, we now need to look at how do they work. Due to you'll quickly find they work very differently compared to undergraduate degrees, so understanding the difference could be a critical factor in helping you to determine if this is something you want to do or not.

How Do Masters Degrees Work?

Originally this blog post was meant to be a very nuanced look at how Masters degrees work, and I planned to look at the main differences between them and undergraduates degrees and things like that. But I was talking to the editor of this blog because he's done a Masters degree, and I very quickly realised that wasn't going to work because I hadn't known how many types of Masters there were. So I had to zoom out a little, so if you want to learn more about the types of Masters degrees then this is definitely the post for you!

Also there will be a mini-interview at the bottom with someone who has actually done a Masters (and done very well at it too) for some tips.

Why Look At Different Masters Degrees?

If this was a blog that was dedicated to one subject area, for example psychology in the case of my podcast, then I could honestly do what I was going to do in the first place. But since this blog is aimed at students from so many subjects, I believe it's important to see what options you have as an undergraduate student.

Due to you might believe there is only one or two set options for you in your subject area, but as I found out the other day there are always options you didn't know about. That's why it's important to look at, so you know what is available to you, and you'll probably find the newly-discovered option might be a better fit for you.

Anything's possible.

What Are The Different Types of Degrees?

As this is a slightly more general post we aren't going to cover subject-specific Masters. For example, the specialised degrees from Law, Business, Art and other subjects. Instead we're going to cover the more general Masters which can be applied in a range of subjects.

For instance, the three most common Masters Degrees are Master of Arts, Master of Science and Master of Research. Which when grouped together I think sound like some strange military ranks, but these are the three I'll give an overview of for you.

What Is A Master of Science?

This I think is the most common to be because these programmes make up the majority of the options available in the social sciences, hard sciences, maths and engineering, and these are the subjects I'm more familiar with. As well as there are massive differences between a Master of Science and Arts.

In addition, a Master of Science focuses on the scientific method, logic and research with these degrees tending to be taught (meaning there are lectures, exams and similar things) over the course of one or two years depending on your subject.

I know from personal experience that clinical psychology degrees, which is what I want to do, is a Master of Science because it focuses on the scientific method, evidence and logic then applies it to mental health and related matters. As well as there are plenty of core modules that are taught to you to help you become more specialise in that area over the course of one year.

That's just one practical example of how a Master of Science is structured. As well as it is worth noting that the academic year for Masters students (regardless of the type) can be longer than undergraduate. Since some Masters are for an academic year (late September to Mid-June) or they can actually be twelve months.

Overall, if you're studying a subject where scientific rigour and research is the focus then a

Master of Science would be a very good idea to study. Since it allows you to deepen your research skills, become more specialised in a specific area and it helps you move on to the next stage. I'll talk more about that in a moment.

What Is A Master of Arts?

If my grandad was reading this he would have a heart attack at what I'm about to say next, but a Master of Arts and Science can be compared ever so slightly, at least until we get into the nitty-gritty.

Due to like Master of Science, a Master of Arts is a taught programme lasting one or two years and the arts, the humanities and some social sciences use Master of Arts. Yet that is where the similarities ends because whereas the Master of Science focuses on logic, the scientific method and research. This one does not.

As the Cambridge Dictionary defines this type of degree as **"an advanced college or university degree in a subject such as literature, language, history, or social science,"** so as you can see this focuses more on cultural and social aspects of the world that cannot be studied empirically.

This makes it perfect for students who want to learn languages, deepen their understanding of areas of history and discuss the work of Shakespeare. But this is far from perfect for other students that need to be research based.

Personally, I remember my cousin doing an MA and me and the rest of my family never actually understood what she did. We did honestly try to understand, but she kept saying she wanted to research aspects of the theatre. Yet we couldn't understand why she didn't do a Master of Science, so she had the empirical knowledge and research skills and then research this area. As well as even now as an undergraduate I try to talk to her about research and despite her completing her MA, I still know a lot more about research skills than her.

So… take of that what you will.

Overall, Master of Arts is a great choice for students who don't want to study science-based subjects, and want to study literature, language and history topics. Yet if science is for you, then definitely do a Master of Science. It would be a lot more useful.

<u>The Differences Between A Master of Science And Art:</u>

In addition to their different focuses, another critical difference between the two types is a Master of Art is what's known as a terminal degree. This means this is the highest level of achievement in a subject, and then a very, very small number of people might choose to do a PhD in the subject. But the vast majority of people do finish higher education with a Master of Art.

For example, a Master of Art in the French language is relatively common in certain circles, but a PhD (and therefore Doctor) of the French Language is exceptionally rare.

On the other hand, Master of Science students

tend to see a Masters as a stepping stone degree towards a PhD. I know that's how things are seen in psychology and others sciences as most of our jobs require a PhD, at least for the really good jobs.

What is A Master of Research?

This is basically the type of degree that shattered my ideas for this blog post because I only learnt about this type a few days ago at the time of writing. However, whilst I cannot say too much on this, the mini-interview at the bottom gives a bit more clarity on this type.

Therefore, a Master of Research applies to all subjects and the focus of the degree is researching an area you want to investigate. There are no deadlines for the course except the final deadlines where the project is due (at least in the research programme) and this type of Masters lasts for one to two years.

Moreover, this type can be divided into two further subtypes. Since a Master of Research can be strictly a research programme like the editor of the blog did, or it can be taught. This I've seen a little bit because there are degrees that focus completely on how to be a better researcher, probably in preparation for people who want to work in academia.

Conclusion:

I know I've probably given you a lot to think about but I want to help you by mentioning this: at the end of the day, there are positives and negatives to all types of Masters. One is not necessarily better than the other and they require intense focus and study. But each type of degree is better for a certain career goal.

Now you have this information in mind, bear in mind the type of Masters degree that will help you in your future career. That is where the critical decision and factors lay, so make sure you choose a degree that is in the best interest for your future.

<u>The Mini-Interview</u>

To give you even more interesting information about Masters degrees, I did a quick interview the other day with the great editor of this blog, Oliver Herdson for his experience of doing a Masters. I found it rather interesting to read, learn from and he gives some great tips.

Enjoy!

1. What was your Masters in?

My masters was a research programme (MSc-Research [MSc-R]). This means it is not a taught programme, so I had no lectures (other than stats). For my research, I elected to explore the role of sad music on emotion and depression.

2. What surprised you about your Masters compared to undergraduate degree?

The independence definitely surprised me. I also took on 3 final year project students (undergraduates) to supervise, and so I found myself surprised by my ability to take on this role.

3. How do you think a Masters compares to an Undergraduate?

My masters was very different, due to it being a research programme. You can think of it as a mini PhD. So, I had a lot more independence and a lot more responsibility. With no lectures or deadlines (apart from the final deadline), my organisation was my own responsibility. It's basically like taking on the final year project on a much larger scale.

4. What tips would you give students looking to do a Masters?

Definitely make the most of your time. Especially if you do a research programme, find some relevant volunteering or work experience to do on the side. For taught programmes, just keep on top of your own organisation and work load.

Quick Wrap-Up

The reason why I like this interview is because it really does highlight some important aspects to bear in mind when choosing a Masters degree, especially a Master of Research. As well as the interview helps with expectation setting and it highlights some of the skills you might need to start working on now so you're a little more prepared for it.

CHAPTER 8

Moving onto our final possible option, I really want to look at PhDs and because the introduction for this chapter is really strong I don't want to keep you from it.

All I'll say is definitely read it, check it out and maybe even try to explore this option a little bit. Since as psychology students this can be an extremely valuable qualification to have if it is something you want.

Why Do A PhD?

Every so often I decide to do what I call "selfish chapters" which are chapters that will help you and you can definitely learn from. But I decide to do them more out of my own curiosity rather than anything else. Personally as an undergraduate student (at the time of writing), I am sort of wondering about the future and I wanted to do a deep dive into the world of doing PhDs, and most importantly why might you want to do one in the first place? So if you're curious definitely read on and let's learn together!

Note: as always none of this blog is ever meant to be professional, career or any sort of official advice.

Why Do A PhD?

Reach Your Career Goals

This is definitely the reason that popped into my mind first because PhDs can be great in certain careers. For example, as a psychology student who wants to go into clinical psychology (just think mental health) I know that becoming a doctor of clinical psychology opens up a lot more doors compared to just doing a Masters' degree.

In addition, this applies to lots of different professions, so if you're currently studying in a profession where being a doctor is important. Then maybe it is worth considering doing a PhD to allow yourself to get access to those higher positions. For example, most hard and social sciences need a very advanced degree (like a PhD) to get access to the high paying jobs, so definitely do have a look.

Learn Transferable Skills

This is probably the only other main reason I could think of by myself, because PhDs really are a lot more than just writing up a massive boring academic paper. Since you get to improve your research skills even further because you have to make an original and important contribution to your subject area with your PhD, so you need to be great at research to do that.

However, there are other, more transferable skills

you can develop because of your PhD. Granted this depends on your subject area, but each one has its own unique skills that you can learn and still benefit from even if you don't decide to work in your chosen area.

For example, from conversations with the great editor of this blog, I know he's doing some teaching alongside his PhD as a part-time job. Now I'm including it in this section because without him doing his PhD, I do not know if he would have gone or gotten this part-time job. Yet because he has it, he is learning teaching, communication and other skills that can help him in other settings if he decided to leave psychology research.

Also as we all know, it takes a lot of skill to explain massive university-level concepts and teach them to undergraduates effectively. I'm still impressed when some teaching assistants manage to explain statistics to us. So I can only applaud everyone who does teaching.

In addition, on a more personal level, I know that the clinical psychology PhDs contain a LOT of fieldwork where we get to work with children and adolescents, working aged adults, retired people and people with learning disabilities. Therefore, this allows us to get tons of practical skills about working with these different groups with their own needs. As a result, there are a wide range of skills developed that I could develop during this PhD that I could use in non-psychology settings.

Overall, you will learn additional skills during your PhD that will help you to become more employable even if you decide to leave your subject area.

Passion And Making A Contribution

Originally meant to be two separate reasons to do a PhD, these advanced forms of degree can be brilliant for people who are passionate about a particular topic within a subject area. Personally as an undergraduate who is currently panicking about choosing a dissertation topic, I do not have any areas of psychology that I am so passionate about that I can think about researching for years.

However, I know that plenty of people even at undergraduate level who are passionate about a particular topic or area within their degree. As well as normally 99% of Masters students have a favourite topic too, so a PhD can be great to explore your passion at an even deeper level.

Also with a PhD you're meant to make an original contribution to your field and doing this in an area you're passionate about makes it a lot easier. Since if you're writing a 60,000 word thesis, believe me you do not want to be doing that on something you hate, so a passionate area is very, very wise indeed.

The only thing I will say is if you're doing a PhD, please find a nice easy to understand way to explain your topic to people outside of your area! Not so much that it will help you during your PhD but it will help those around you understand what you're doing.

Moreover, making an original contribution can be a great opportunity for you to help your career during your PhD. You only need to look on the internet to find names of researchers and academics who started to make a name for themselves during their PhD. Of course, it might not happen to you and chances are it won't, but it never hurts to try.

On the whole, if you have an area you're passionate about and really want to explore in great depth. Then a PhD can allow you to do that, and if you can make an original contribution to your field then that is amazing too!

Conclusion:

Before this post I definitely felt like PhDs were this more mythical area of higher education, because people talk about them, but never in any great depth. Especially they don't really talk about why do one. Yet hopefully after this blog post, you now have enough information to start thinking if there's a chance you might want to do a PhD in the future.

There are benefits. But remember you don't have to do it. It is always your choice.

Remember that and you'll be fine.

HOW DO PHDS WORK?

For our final chapter, I suppose it wouldn't really be right unless I went all out for it. So in this final chapter we really get a good and rather deep understanding of how PhDs work.

As well as there is a wonderful mini-interview from a psychology student currently starting his PhD and this chapter is definitely worth it for that interview alone, as it really helps to bring the topic alive.

So let's learn how PhDs work!

How Do PhDs Work?

This is probably one of the hardest blog posts I have ever had to write (and I've written at least 200 posts) because trying to write about how a PhD works is like trying to explain how different cars work. There are so many different types, but thankfully for us there are some core principles that most PhDs have. Granted if you do medicine, psychology and other subject areas, there will be differences for you. Yet this post will still be very useful and there is a mini-interview at the bottom from a current PhD student.

Keep reading to learn more!

Note: whilst this is a very UK-centric post, most countries do follow this format and information with subtle differences. For instance, in the United States, students complete reading assignments and examinations before beginning their research.

What Is A PhD?

In case you aren't familiar with what a PhD is, it is a type of doctorate that stands for Doctor of Philosophy. As well as unlike the vast majority of Masters and all undergraduate programs, a PhD is strictly a research programme.

Well, that is only true to a certain point as you'll see in the mini-interview and I know different subjects have different requirements.

However, this is why modern PhDs are much more diverse and interesting compared to the more traditional ones, where you literally do just spend three to four years researching and doing nothing else.

Additionally, it might be worth checking out my Why Do A PhD? Post if you want to learn more about some of the benefits of doing this type of degree in the first place.

How Do PhDs Work?

As I mentioned earlier, this next section will be very general and for the sake of awareness, I will do a smaller section afterwards that explains some of the differences between what is mentioned here and other degrees. Like my own clinical psychology.

A typical PhD involves carrying out a professional literature review, which is a massive survey of the current studies and literature in your field. For example, earlier in the academic year for my psychology placement, I did a literature review on mobile mental health apps, so I looked at studies discussing this area to find the general trends of the literature. That's the easiest way to explain it.

In addition, and most importantly, you conduct original research that will help advance the field you're looking at and you collect your results. Then you produce a thesis presenting your conclusions.

Afterwards you write up and submit your thesis as your dissertation (about a 60,000 word report).

Then you get the very fun job of defending your thesis in an oral "viva voce" exam.

I forget why but I did look up those oral exams years ago and they sound... interesting to say the least. Since as far as I know they are designed to test you and chances are you will be given an improvement or two to make before they officially pass you. But as far as I know by the time you got to this stage, failing your PhD should be very rare.

But don't quote me on that, as well as we do briefly cover this type of examination in a later section.

Overall, whilst these areas do differ from degree to degree these are the major things you will have to do as part of your PhD.

Brief Overview of What Happens In Each Year In A PhD:

In terms of what actually happens in each year of a PhD, it works as you could expect if we fellow those five things in the section above.

The First Year of A PhD:

Therefore, in your first year, you would meet with your PhD supervisor and discuss an action plan for your research proposal. Following that you would complete your literature review, using guidance from your supervisor. This will allow you to know the gaps in the literature, justify your study (why is it needed in the first place) and it will help you to make your work original.

Then towards the end of the first year, you start to begin your own research by designing experiments and you might have time to start researching.

The Second Year of A PhD:

In the second year, this is where you do most of your research. As well as this is where most of the differences happen between the different subjects, but the main focus for this year would be gathering results from experiments, surveys or whatever research you are doing.

Subsequently, as your research develops, you would come up with your thesis (also known as argument) you will base your dissertation on. Then you might start writing up chapters or other pieces that will form part of your dissertation in the future.

Personally, the idea of academically writing chapters is just frightening. Writing for that long in an academic style would be a struggle. But I'm mentioning this in case any other readers who are thinking about doing a PhD and are thinking about their academic writing, know that they aren't alone. And most importantly, you do have years to perfect your writing style before you get there.

And chances are (an almost certainly) is if you get to do a PhD, then your academic writing is excellent.

However, during all of this, you will be having regular meetings with your supervisor and this year is critical for your development as a scholar. Due to you would already be very well versed in current research, how to do research and write up research, but you wouldn't be an "expert" in scholarly things yet.

That's why at this point in your PhD (and because it is arguably the non-busiest time), it is a good idea to think about presenting work at academic conferences, gaining teaching experience and maybe even select some material for publication in an academic journal. There are other examples but you could possibly say it is critical to try and get more than a PhD during these years.

As explained in the mini-interview section in a moment.

The Third/ Four Year:

During your final year, the main focus is apparently to simply write up and hone your thesis into a dissertation. Yet the reality is far less simple from that because it is not uncommon for PhD students to still be fine-tuning experiments, chasing up a few extra sources and collecting results. This is very likely if your second year is focused on professional development.

Then you will have to submit your dissertation and go onto the viva voce oral exams. Which is a formal discussion and defence of your thesis involving at least one internal and external examiner. Thankfully it is normally the only assessment in a PhD and once you've passed it, you are done.

Differences Between Subjects and Conclusion

To wrap up this blog post, I want to emphasise that you do investigate how PhDs work in the subject area you love, study and want to work in. There will be differences. For example, in clinical psychology, we have to work with the 4 clinical populations so we have work experience working with all the types of people could encounter as a clinical psychologist. Then I know business and law have their requirements too.

PhDs aren't meant to scary, impossible things that people have sleepiness nights over. Are they hard? Definitely.

But they can be worth it for people who want to become doctors and basically experts in their fields, in addition to the other benefits I discuss in *Why Do A PhD?*.

I hope this has increased your awareness of PhDs (I know I have) and maybe even inspired you to do the same.

Because, come on, who doesn't want to be called *Doctor*?

Mini-Interview on PhDs With Oliver Herdson

As I did on the *How Do Masters Degree Work?* Post, I asked the great editor of this blog Oliver Herdson some questions to help give the post a bit of *lived experience*. A massive thank you to Oliver for his help.

What is your PhD in?

My PhD is cognitive and neuropsychology – I'm looking at the underlying cognitive mechanisms of depression

What surprised you about your PhD compared to undergraduate and Masters degree?

In my particular instance, I got a PhD on a scholarship so I became staff as well as a student – which of course is quite the adjustment. In a general sense though, again it is the independence and responsibility that is the big difference. Also, becoming more like peers with your supervisor (if you're lucky to have that relationship with your supervisor) is a nice experience.

How have you found your first year so far?

I've really liked it, I've struggled to keep on top of everything as it does get very busy at times. Overall though, I've learnt so much already.

What tips would you give students looking to do a PhD?

Tip 1 is look for scholarships. There's a lot of different routes to go and securing funding is much easier on you financially.

Tip 2 would be to plan your research early — have a clear idea of what you want to research. The likelihood is that your research will get turned on its head in the first few months, so starting as early as possible is important.

CONCLUSION

After reading this book, I really hope that a lot of your university questions have been answered about how it all works, what you need to think about before you go to university and then during and beyond.

University can be an amazing time in your life if you put effort into and that's another point of the (so far) three guides in this series.

This guide looked at how it all worked, and if you want to learn more then I highly recommend checking out *A Student's Guide To University And Learning* and *University Mental Health and Mindset*. As both of these will really help you to develop your knowledge of university further. As well as both of them are filled with plenty of useful tips to help you hopefully thrive at university.

Next Steps:

I really like to finish off these guides by suggesting some unofficial next steps for you to help you further. Therefore, in this book, I have the following three to suggest.

Firstly, I would definitely make sure that you know a lot about your university before you make your final choice about where to go. I know this might not be applicable to all readers as you might have chosen it already.

However, you're going to be spending at least three years of your life at university so you might as well make sure it's going to be fun, interesting and it will cater to your interests.

Of course, you won't know for sure until you actually get there and start exploring university life, but you should have a good idea by looking at their website and listening to the experiences of other students.

And believe me, in this case YouTube is your friend. The vast majority of universities have at least one or two students that are YouTubers and they tend to give reviews of the university after they're left.

Find them!

Some of them can be extremely interesting.

Secondly, keep learning. Not so much how does university work because we really have covered most of it in this book but keep learning about how to prepare for university. Since some students need that more than others.

Finally, as I mentioned earlier check out the other books in the series. Lots of people have found the blog posts these books are based on to be very useful and helpful.

You can learn a lot about university life through them, and they're available from wherever you bought this book from.

I just want to leave with you by saying that I truly do love university, I love the opportunities it has given me and I cannot encourage you enough to try and make the most of university.

You'll be surprised at where it can take you if you network, have fun and take advantage of opportunities. And funnily enough they're all topics in the *A Student's Guide To University And Learning*.

Have a great day and hopefully I'll see you in another book soon.

https://www.subscribepage.com/psychologyboxset

Thank you for reading.
I hoped you enjoyed it.
If you want a FREE book and keep up to date about new books and project. Then please sign up for my newsletter at
www.connorwhiteley.net/
Have a great day.

CHECK OUT THE PSYCHOLOGY WORLD PODCAST FOR MORE PSYCHOLOGY INFORMATION! AVAILABLE ON ALL MAJOR PODCAST APPS.

About the author:

Connor Whiteley is the author of over 60 books in the sci-fi fantasy, nonfiction psychology and books for writer's genre and he is a Human Branding Speaker and Consultant.

He is a passionate warhammer 40,000 reader, psychology student and author.

Who narrates his own audiobooks and he hosts The Psychology World Podcast.

All whilst studying Psychology at the University of Kent, England.

Also, he was a former Explorer Scout where he gave a speech to the Maltese President in August 2018 and he attended Prince Charles' 70th Birthday Party at Buckingham Palace in May 2018.

Plus, he is a self-confessed coffee lover!

HOW DOES UNIVERSITY WORK?

All books in 'An Introductory Series':
BIOLOGICAL PSYCHOLOGY 3RD EDITION
COGNITIVE PSYCHOLOGY THIRD EDITION
SOCIAL PSYCHOLOGY- 3RD EDITION
ABNORMAL PSYCHOLOGY 3RD EDITION
PSYCHOLOGY OF RELATIONSHIPS- 3RD EDITION
DEVELOPMENTAL PSYCHOLOGY 3RD EDITION
HEALTH PSYCHOLOGY
RESEARCH IN PSYCHOLOGY
A GUIDE TO MENTAL HEALTH AND TREATMENT AROUND THE WORLD- A GLOBAL LOOK AT DEPRESSION
FORENSIC PSYCHOLOGY
THE FORENSIC PSYCHOLOGY OF THEFT, BURGLARY AND OTHER CRIMES AGAINST PROPERTY
CRIMINAL PROFILING: A FORENSIC PSYCHOLOGY GUIDE TO FBI PROFILING AND GEOGRAPHICAL AND STATISTICAL PROFILING.
CLINICAL PSYCHOLOGY
FORMULATION IN PSYCHOTHERAPY

PERSONALITY PSYCHOLOGY AND INDIVIDUAL DIFFERENCES
CLINICAL PSYCHOLOGY REFLECTIONS VOLUME 1
CLINICAL PSYCHOLOGY REFLECTIONS VOLUME 2
CULT PSYCHOLOGY
Police Psychology

A Psychology Student's Guide To University
How Does University Work?
A Student's Guide To University And Learning
University Mental Health and Mindset

HOW DOES UNIVERSITY WORK?

<u>Companion guides:</u>
<u>BIOLOGICAL PSYCHOLOGY 2ND EDITION WORKBOOK</u>
<u>COGNITIVE PSYCHOLOGY 2ND EDITION WORKBOOK</u>
<u>SOCIOCULTURAL PSYCHOLOGY 2ND EDITION WORKBOOK</u>
<u>ABNORMAL PSYCHOLOGY 2ND EDITION WORKBOOK</u>
<u>PSYCHOLOGY OF HUMAN RELATIONSHIPS 2ND EDITION WORKBOOK</u>
<u>HEALTH PSYCHOLOGY WORKBOOK</u>
<u>FORENSIC PSYCHOLOGY WORKBOOK</u>

OTHER SHORT STORIES BY CONNOR WHITELEY

<u>Mystery Short Stories:</u>
Poison In The Candy Cane
Christmas Innocence
You Better Watch Out
Christmas Theft
Trouble In Christmas
Smell of The Lake
Problem In A Car
Theft, Past and Team
Embezzler In The Room
A Strange Way To Go
A Horrible Way To Go
Ann Awful Way To Go
An Old Way To Go
A Fishy Way To Go
A Pointy Way To Go
A High Way To Go
A Fiery Way To Go
A Glassy Way To Go
A Chocolatey Way To Go
Kendra Detective Mystery Collection Volume 1
Kendra Detective Mystery Collection Volume 2
Stealing A Chance At Freedom

Glassblowing and Death
Theft of Independence
Cookie Thief
Marble Thief
Book Thief
Art Thief
Mated At The Morgue
The Big Five Whoopee Moments
Stealing An Election
Mystery Short Story Collection Volume 1
Mystery Short Story Collection Volume 2

Science Fiction Short Stories:
The First Rememberer
Life of A Rememberer
System of Wonder
Lifesaver
Remarkable Way She Died
The Interrogation of Annabella Stormic
Blade of The Emperor
Arbiter's Truth
Computation of Battle
Old One's Wrath
Puppets and Masters
Ship of Plague
Interrogation
Edge of Failure

One Way Choice
Acceptable Losses
Balance of Power
Good Idea At The Time
Escape Plan
Escape In The Hesitation
Inspiration In Need
Singing Warriors
Knowledge is Power
Killer of Polluters
Climate of Death
The Family Mailing Affair
Defining Criminality
The Martian Affair
A Cheating Affair
The Little Café Affair
Mountain of Death
Prisoner's Fight
Claws of Death
Bitter Air
Honey Hunt
Blade On A Train

HOW DOES UNIVERSITY WORK?

<u>Fantasy Short Stories:</u>
City of Snow
City of Light
City of Vengeance
Dragons, Goats and Kingdom
Smog The Pathetic Dragon
Don't Go In The Shed
The Tomato Saver
The Remarkable Way She Died
The Bloodied Rose
Asmodia's Wrath
Heart of A Killer
Emissary of Blood
Dragon Coins
Dragon Tea
Dragon Rider
Sacrifice of the Soul
Heart of The Flesheater
Heart of The Regent
Heart of The Standing
Feline of The Lost
Heart of The Story
City of Fire
Awaiting Death

Other books by Connor Whiteley:
Bettie English Private Eye Series
A Very Private Woman
The Russian Case
A Very Urgent Matter
A Case Most Personal
Trains, Scots and Private Eyes
The Federation Protects

The Fireheart Fantasy Series
Heart of Fire
Heart of Lies
Heart of Prophecy
Heart of Bones
Heart of Fate

City of Assassins (Urban Fantasy)
City of Death
City of Marytrs
City of Pleasure
City of Power

Agents of The Emperor
Return of The Ancient Ones
Vigilance
Angels of Fire
Kingmaker

HOW DOES UNIVERSITY WORK?

<u>The Garro Series- Fantasy/Sci-fi</u>
GARRO: GALAXY'S END
GARRO: RISE OF THE ORDER
GARRO: END TIMES
GARRO: SHORT STORIES
GARRO: COLLECTION
GARRO: HERESY
GARRO: FAITHLESS
GARRO: DESTROYER OF WORLDS
GARRO: COLLECTIONS BOOK 4-6
GARRO: MISTRESS OF BLOOD
GARRO: BEACON OF HOPE
GARRO: END OF DAYS

<u>Winter Series- Fantasy Trilogy Books</u>
WINTER'S COMING
WINTER'S HUNT
WINTER'S REVENGE
WINTER'S DISSENSION

<u>Miscellaneous:</u>
RETURN
FREEDOM
SALVATION
Reflection of Mount Flame
The Masked One
The Great Deer

Audiobooks by Connor Whiteley:
BIOLOGICAL PSYCHOLOGY
COGNITIVE PSYCHOLOGY
SOCIOCULTURAL PSYCHOLOGY
ABNORMAL PSYCHOLOGY
PSYCHOLOGY OF HUMAN RELATIONSHIPS
HEALTH PSYCHOLOGY
DEVELOPMENTAL PSYCHOLOGY
RESEARCH IN PSYCHOLOGY
FORENSIC PSYCHOLOGY
GARRO: GALAXY'S END
GARRO: RISE OF THE ORDER
GARRO: SHORT STORIES
GARRO: END TIMES
GARRO: COLLECTION
GARRO: HERESY
GARRO: FAITHLESS
GARRO: DESTROYER OF WORLDS
GARRO: COLLECTION BOOKS 4-6
GARRO: COLLECTION BOOKS 1-6

Business books:
TIME MANAGEMENT: A GUIDE FOR STUDENTS AND WORKERS
LEADERSHIP: WHAT MAKES A GOOD LEADER? A GUIDE FOR STUDENTS AND WORKERS.
BUSINESS SKILLS: HOW TO SURVIVE THE BUSINESS WORLD? A GUIDE FOR STUDENTS, EMPLOYEES AND EMPLOYERS.
BUSINESS COLLECTION

GET YOUR FREE BOOK AT:
WWW.CONNORWHITELEY.NET

www.ingramcontent.com/pod-product-compliance
Lightning Source LLC
LaVergne TN
LVHW012112070526
838202LV00056B/5698